The Book of JONAH

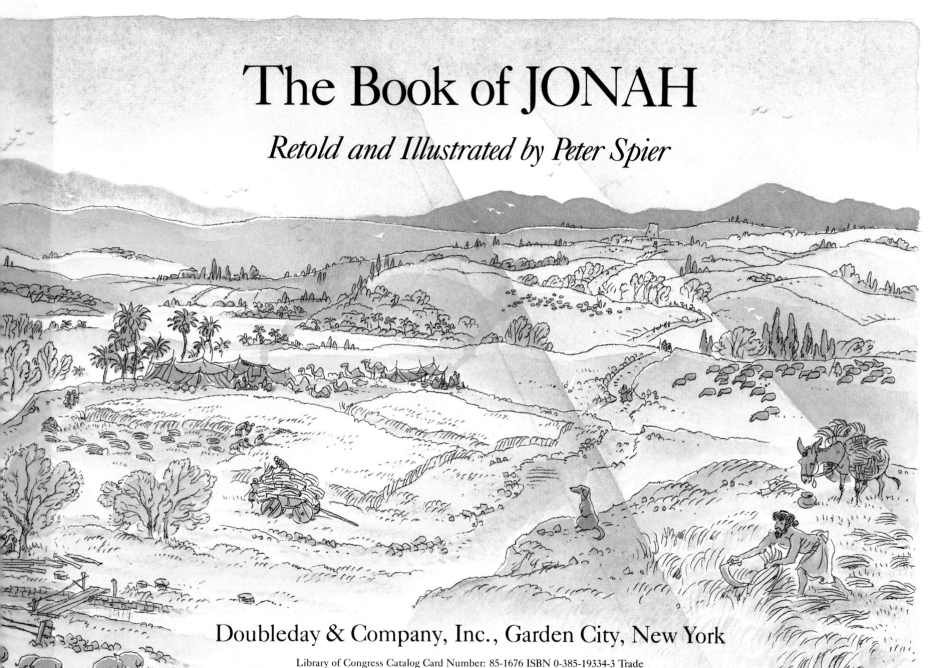

The Book of JONAH

Retold and Illustrated by Peter Spier

Doubleday & Company, Inc., Garden City, New York

Library of Congress Catalog Card Number: 85-1676 ISBN 0-385-19334-3 Trade
ISBN 0-385-19335-1 Prebound Text and Illustrations Copyright © 1985 by Peter Spier
All Rights Reserved Printed in the United States of America First Edition

And the Lord said to Jonah, "Get up, go to the city of Nineveh, and speak out against it, for its evil ways have offended me."

But instead, Jonah decided to flee from the Lord.

He went to Joppa, found a ship bound for Tarshish
(far away, in the opposite direction of Nineveh),
paid the fare, and went on board.

They said to him, "Tell us, please, why has this evil befallen us? What is your occupation, and where do you come from? What is your country, and to which people do you belong?"

And Jonah said to them, "I am a Hebrew. I worship the Lord, the God of Heaven, who made the sea and the dry land."

Then the men were very frightened, and said to him, "What have you done?" For they knew that he was fleeing from the Lord, because he had told them so.

They said to him, "What shall we do to calm the sea?" For the storm was still increasing, and the waves rose ever higher.

And he said to them, "Take me and throw me into the sea, because only then will the sea be calm again. For I know that it is because of me that this storm is upon you."

Instead, the men rowed hard to reach the safety of land, but could not, for the waves rose higher and higher against them.

Then the Lord sent a great wind onto the sea, creating a mighty storm, which threatened to break up the ship.

The seamen were afraid, and each cried out to his own god, and they threw the ship's cargo into the sea to lighten their vessel.

But Jonah had gone down below into the hold, where he had fallen fast asleep.

And the captain came to him, saying, "What is the matter with you? Get up, call upon your God. Maybe your God will take notice of us, and not let us perish."

Then the seamen said to each other, "Come, let us cast lots to discover who is responsible for the evil that has come upon us."

So they cast lots, and the lot fell upon Jonah.

Therefore they cried to the Lord, and said, "We beg of you, do not let us perish because of this man's sin, and do not punish us for taking this man's life. For you, Lord, are responsible for this; you have done as you pleased." So they picked up Jonah, and threw him into the sea. And the sea stopped its raging, and grew calm.

This frightened the seamen greatly; so they offered a sacrifice, and made solemn promises to the Lord.

Now, the Lord had arranged for a great fish to swallow Jonah. And Jonah was in the belly of the fish for three days and three nights.

Jonah prayed to the Lord, his God, from the belly of the fish, saying that he was deeply sorry to have disobeyed, and begging for forgiveness and mercy.

He ended his prayer by saying, "I shall sacrifice to you with the voice of thanksgiving. What I have promised I shall do. Salvation belongs to the Lord." And the Lord spoke to the fish, and it vomited Jonah out onto dry land.

Then the word of the Lord came to Jonah a second time, saying, "Get up, go to the city of Nineveh, and warn them of their doom as I told you to do before."

Jonah arose and went to Nineveh, according to the
word of the Lord; a journey of three days.

When he reached the city, he entered it, and walked around in it for a day, warning, "In forty days Nineveh shall be destroyed!"

And the people of Nineveh believed Jonah, and proclaimed a fast, and put on rough sackcloth, from the greatest to the very least of them.

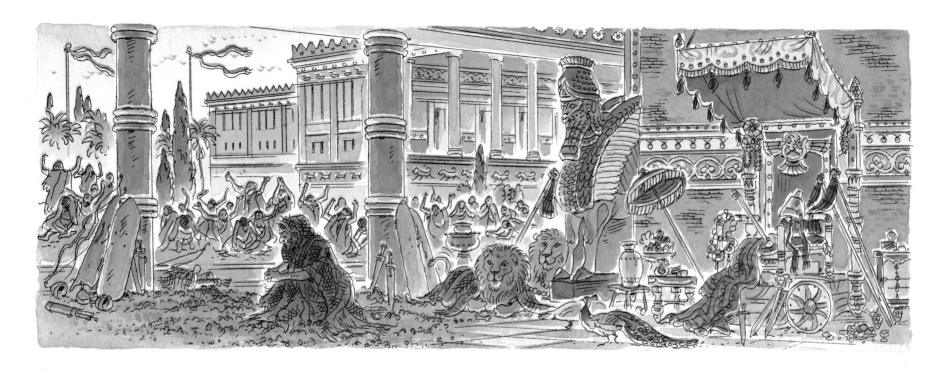

The word also reached the King of Nineveh. He got up from his throne, took off his magnificent robe, and covered himself with sackcloth, and sat down among the ashes.

And the King and his nobles decreed, "Let neither man nor beast, ox nor sheep, eat anything; do not let them graze, or drink water, but let man and beast be covered with sackcloth, and pray to God with all their might. They shall all turn from their evil ways and violence."

"Who knows, God may yet reconsider, and turn his anger from us, so that we will not perish."

When God saw what they were doing, he regretted the punishment he had promised to send upon them, and he did not do it.

But this displeased Jonah very much, and he was very angry. He prayed to the Lord, saying, "O Lord, did I not predict this when I was still in my own country? That is why I fled to Tarshish. For I knew that you are a gracious and merciful God, slow to anger, and of great kindness. I knew that you would change your mind.

"Therefore, O Lord, take away my life, for it is better for me to die than to live."

And the Lord replied, saying, "Are you right to be this angry?"

Jonah left the city, and went out to the east side of it.

He built a shelter for himself, sat down, and waited to see what would become of the city.

And God provided a vine, made it grow up over Jonah's head so that he would be shaded, and to soothe his anger.

And Jonah rejoiced greatly in the vine. But at sunrise the next day, God sent a worm which chewed through the vine, so that it withered.

And when the sun had risen, God arranged a warm east wind, and the sun beat down on Jonah's head, so that he felt faint and wanted to die.

Then God said to Jonah, "What right do you have to be so angry about the vine?" And he answered, "I have every right to be angry, angry enough to die."

The Lord then said to him, "You feel pity for the vine, which you did not plant nor tend, which came up in one night, and perished in one night.

"So should I not feel pity for Nineveh, that great city, in which there are more than one hundred and twenty thousand people who do not know right from wrong, to say nothing of all their animals?"

Modern scholars believe that the Book of Jonah was written between 400 and 200 B.C., and this means that it is far closer to us in time than most of us realize. At that time Jerusalem had been a city for over sixteen centuries, the Egyptian pyramids were 2,200 years old, the Kings David and Solomon had been dead for almost 700 years, and Homer had written the *Iliad* 500 years previously.

There is little doubt that Jonah was a historical figure who lived in Gath-Hepher near Nazareth during the reign of the Israelite King Jeroboam II (c. 789–48 B.C.), and it seems equally certain that the unknown writer used the revered name of Jonah to reinforce the credibility of his story, an "unauthorized endorsement," or teaching of God's concern for all mankind and compassion for those who truly repent.

Some view the story as reliable history, others as a parable, and many Christians believe that Jonah is a prefiguration of Christ, for St. Matthew writes ". . . for as Jonah was three days and three nights in the whale's belly, so shall the Son of man be three days and three nights in the heart of the earth." Jesus considered Jonah's story as fact: ". . . This is an evil generation: they seek a sign; and there shall no sign be given it, but the sign of Jonas the prophet. For as Jonas was a sign unto the Ninevites, so shall also the Son of man be to this generation." (Luke 11:29,30)

Moslems regard Yūnus, "the man of the fish," as one of Allah's apostles, and the Koran, the sacred book of Islam, mentions him in three of the 114 chapters, and one of these bears his name.

In Jonah's time Israel was in the shadow of its mighty neighbor the Assyrian Empire, which covered the territory of present-day Iraq and Syria. We know that Nineveh, which became the capital of Assyria in the eighth century B.C., covered eighteen hundred acres within a wall eight miles long. Diodorus, a historian of the first century B.C., wrote that ". . . its walls were one hundred feet high, with room for three chariots to drive abreast on them, and there were fifteen hundred towers, each two hundred feet in height." It was a city of enormous temples to a variety of gods, filled with palaces, offices and public buildings. Fortifications made the city virtually impregnable, and the aqueduct, the oldest in the world, supplied water from thirty miles away. A botanical garden contained every tree, plant and bush, fruit and flower growing in the empire.

So it seems small wonder that Jonah, aside from having to journey the 550 miles from Joppa to Nineveh, was fearful and reluctant when ordered to go to that sophisticated and most magnificent of cities, the very symbol of world power, to tell them of their impending doom.

Joppa, today's Jaffa, a suburb of Tel Aviv in Israel, which lies thirty-five miles to northwest of Jerusalem, was a thriving port when Jonah lived and had been since ancient times. Much later it was in Joppa that St. Peter stayed at the house of Simon the tanner and raised Tabitha from the dead.

Jonah must have chosen to escape to the most distant place he could think of—and Tarshish was just that, a Phoenician colony 2,300 miles away on the southern coast of Spain, at the very western edge of the world known to the peoples of the ancient Near East. Tarshish was most likely the city of Tartessos, although not all scholars agree. Jonah was no doubt familiar with Tarshish, for in I Kings it states ". . . for the king had at sea a fleet of Tarshish with the navy of Hiram: once in three years came the navy of Tarshish, bringing gold, and silver, ivory, and apes, and peacocks."

MAP OF NINEVEH'S RUINS TODAY

1. City wall
2. Eastern gate
3. North gate
4. City moat
5. Outer walls and moats
6. Aqueduct to Jerwan
7. Ancient riverbed of Tigris
8. Khoser River
9. Mound of Quyunjiq
10. Library
11. Palace of Sennacherib
12. Palace of Ashurbanipal
13. Cemetery and Nebi Yūnus
14. Villages
15. Roads and paths
16. Road to Khorsabad

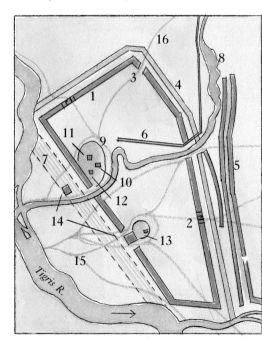

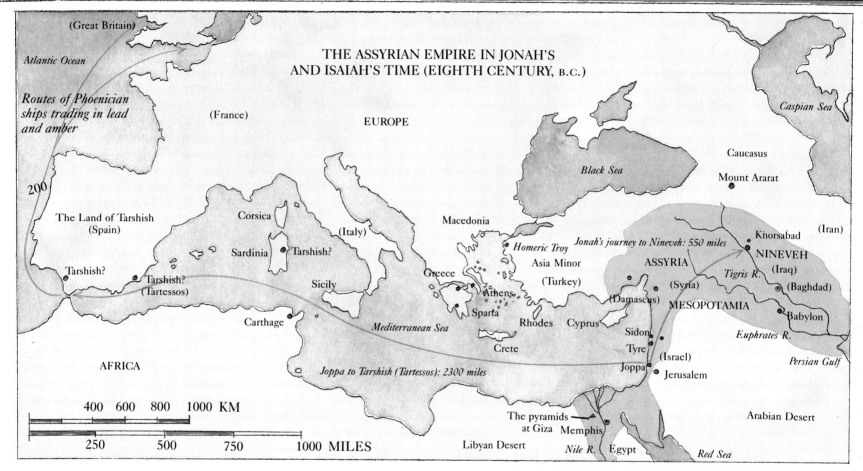

THE ASSYRIAN EMPIRE IN JONAH'S
AND ISAIAH'S TIME (EIGHTH CENTURY, B.C.)

(Great Britain)

Atlantic Ocean

*Routes of Phoenician
ships trading in lead
and amber*

(France)

EUROPE

Caspian Sea

200

Corsica

Black Sea

Caucasus

Mount Ararat

The Land of Tarshish
(Spain)

Sardinia   Tarshish?

(Italy)

Macedonia

Homeric Troy

Asia Minor

Jonah's journey to Nineveh: 550 miles   Khorsabad   (Iran)

NINEVEH

Tarshish?   Tarshish?
(Tartessos)

Sicily

Greece

(Turkey)

ASSYRIA

Tigris R.   (Iraq)

(Syria)

(Baghdad)

Athens

(Damascus)   MESOPOTAMIA

Carthage   *Mediterranean Sea*   Sparta   Rhodes   Cyprus

Sidon   Babylon

Euphrates R.

AFRICA

Crete   Tyre   (Israel)

Joppa   Jerusalem

Persian Gulf

400   600   800   1000 KM

Joppa to Tarshish (Tartessos): 2300 miles

The pyramids
at Giza   Memphis   Arabian Desert

250   500   750   1000 MILES

Libyan Desert   *Nile R.*   Egypt   *Red Sea*

During the seventh century B.C., Assyrian power gradually eroded and that of Babylonia steadily grew. In 612 B.C. the Babylonians and their allies launched their final assault on Nineveh, and the city fell as foretold by the prophets Nahum and Zephaniah.

"And it shall come to pass," prophesied Nahum, "that all they that look upon thee shall flee from thee, and say, Nineveh is laid waste: who will bemoan her?" (Na. 3:7)

And in Zephaniah (2:13–14) we read: "And he will stretch out his hand against the north, and destroy Assyria; and will make Nineveh a desolation, and dry like a wilderness. And flocks shall lie down in the midst of her . . . "

Nineveh was sacked and burned and for twenty-four centuries the curtain of time descended on the dust and rubble of what had been the mightiest city on the face of the earth. And so Jonah finally had his wish.

In the centuries that followed great armies marched through these lands. In

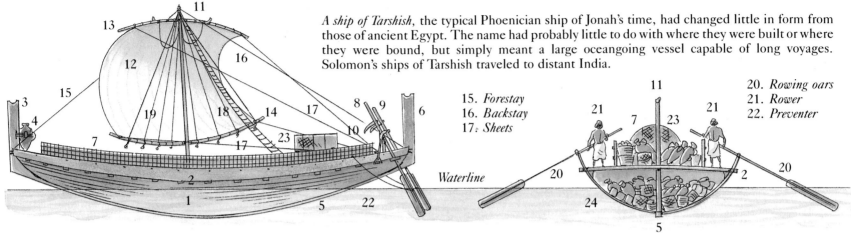

A ship of Tarshish, the typical Phoenician ship of Jonah's time, had changed little in form from those of ancient Egypt. The name had probably little to do with where they were built or where they were bound, but simply meant a large oceangoing vessel capable of long voyages. Solomon's ships of Tarshish traveled to distant India.

15. *Forestay*
16. *Backstay*
17. *Sheets*

20. *Rowing oars*
21. *Rower*
22. *Preventer*

Waterline

1. *Hull*
2. *Protruding deck beams*
3. *Fore-post*
4. *Freshwater barrel*
5. *Keel*
6. *Sternpost*
7. *Fences to contain cargo on deck*

8. *Port steering oar*
9. *Starboard steering oar*
10. *Tillers*
11. *Mast*
12. *Sail*
13. *Topsail yard, two sections lashed together*
14. *Lower yard of two sections*

18. *Rope ladder to masthead*
19. *Halyards*

23. *Shelter on deck*
24. *Cargo hold*

401 B.C. a Greek army retreating to far-off Sparta, after their defeat by the Persians, trudged through the ruins of Nineveh without ever realizing it . . . Alexander the Great and his army passed here as well, and he, too, was never aware that the crumbled bricks, shallow ditches and barren mounds through which his army wound its way had once been "the city at which men marvel . . . " And so it remained for over 2,000 years.

Claudius James Rich of the British East India Company, stationed in Baghdad, was the first to examine the ruins of Nineveh seriously, in 1816. Four years later, having heard rumors that artifacts and strange sculptures, half man, half beast, had been dug up by the natives, he rushed back to the sites, only to find that everything found had been completely smashed on orders of Muslim clergymen as "infidel idols." He left empty-handed without having the slightest idea that the two great mounds on the eastern bank of the Tigris he passed on the way home concealed all that was left of Nineveh. The larger was called Quyunjiq ("Little Lamb"), and contained royal palaces and temples. The other was Nebi Yūnis ("the prophet

The mosque and the traditional Tomb of Jonah, "the man of the fish."